Diary Written in the Provincial Lunatic Asylum

by

Mary Huestis Pengilly

Diary from a Lunatic Asylum

A True Story of Life in an Asylum

ISBN-13:
978-1979322164

ISBN-10:
1979322163

DIARY WRITTEN IN THE
Provincial Lunatic Asylum,

BY

M H PENGILLY

The prison doors are open—I am free;
Be this my messenger o'er land and sea.

PUBLISHED BY THE AUTHOR.
1885.

This little book is humbly dedicated to the Province of New Brunswick, and the State of Massachusetts, by one who has had so sad an experience in this, the sixty-second year of her age, that she feels it to be her imperative duty to lay it before the public in such a manner as shall reach the hearts of the people in this her native Province, as also the people of Massachusetts, with whom she had a refuge since driven from her own home by the St. John fire of 1877. She sincerely hopes it may be read in every State of the Union, as well as throughout the Dominion of Canada, that it may help to show the inner workings of their Hospitals and Asylums, and prompt them to search out better methods of conducting them, as well for the benefit of the superintendent as the patient.

December.—They will not allow me to go home, and I must write these things down for fear I forget. It will help to pass the time away. It is very hard to endure this prison life, and know that my sons think me insane when I am not.

How unkind Mrs. Mills is today; does she think this sort of treatment is for the good of our health? I

begged for milk today, and she can't spare me any;
she has not enough for all the old women, she says.
I don't wish to deprive any one of that which they
require, but have I not a right to all I require to
feed me and make me well? All I do need is good
nourishing food, and I know better than any one
else can what I require to build me up and make
me as I was before I met with this strange change
of condition. I remember telling the Doctor, on his
first visit to my room, that I only needed biscuit and
milk and beef tea to make me well. He rose to his
feet and said, "I know better than any other man."
That was all I heard him say, and he walked out,
leaving me without a word of sympathy, or a
promise that I should have anything. I say to myself
(as I always talk aloud to myself when not well),
"You don't know any more than this old woman
does." I take tea with Mrs. Mills; I don't like to look
at those patients who look so wretched.

I can't bear to see myself in the glass, I am so
wasted—so miserable. My poor boys, no wonder
you look so sad, to see your mother looking so
badly, and be compelled to leave her here alone
among strangers who know nothing about her past
life. They don't seem to have any respect for me. If
I were the most miserable woman in the city of St.
John, I would be entitled to better treatment at the
hands of those who are paid by the Province to
make us as comfortable as they can, by keeping us
warmed and fed, as poor feeble invalids should be
kept.

December 20.—I have made myself quite happy
this week, thinking of what Christmas may bring to
many childish hearts, and how I once tried to make
my own dear boys happy at Christmas time. I
helped poor Maggy to make artificial flowers for a
wreath she herself had made of cedar. She was
making it for some friend in the Asylum. She never
goes out; she wishes to go sometimes, but Mrs.
Mills scolds her a little, then she works on and says
no more about it. Poor Maggy! there is nothing
ailing her but a little too much temper. She does all
the dining-room work—washes dishes and many
other things.

January.—They have had a festival; it was made, I suppose, to benefit some one here; I don't know whom. It certainly did not benefit me any; no one invited me to go to the church where the festival was held, but Dr. Crookshank, the Assistant Physician, looked at me very kindly and said, "Do come, Mrs. Pengilly, you may as well come." I looked at my dress (it is grey flannel, and I have had no other to change since I came here), "I can't go looking like this; I must be a little better dressed to go into a public meeting of any kind; I am not accustomed to go looking like this, with nothing on my neck." He said, "Very well, something shall come to you;" and Mrs. Hays, who is Assistant Nurse in our Ward, brought me a plate of food and fruit, such as is generally had at festivals.

I have not had my trunk yet; sure the boys did not leave me here without my trunk. Perhaps they do not wish me to go in sight of people from the city, for fear they will recognize me, and I should make my complaints known to them. I have entreated them to give me my trunk so many times in vain that I have given it up. I did ask Mrs. Mills, and she says, "Ask Mrs. Murphy, she has charge of the trunk room." I asked her; she says she will see, and she will bring me whatever I need that is in it. She puts me off with a soft answer, until I begin to think there is nothing done for any one here, only what they cannot avoid. It is a self-running establishment, I guess, for no one seems to know how or when to do anything I wish to have done, whatever they may do for others.

February.—The weather is cold. I have more to occupy my time now. I have learned how to let off the cold air from the radiators, and then we get more heat. I do it when no one sees me. I shall do all I can to make myself comfortable, and they all share it. When I arise in the morning, my first thought is to look up the hall to see if there is fire in the grate—the one little grate in that large hall, to give warmth and comfort to us poor prisoners. If the fire is there, I feel pleased; I go up as soon as the sweeping is done, and try to feel at home. I tell the nurse I will tend the fire, if she will have the coal left beside the grate. Sometimes they allow it willingly, and I enjoy it. I brush up the hearth, and make it look cheerful and homelike as possible. I draw up the huge, uncomfortable seats to form a circle; they stand round until I get there; they are happy to sit with me, but they don't know enough to draw up a seat for themselves. I have found pleasure in this; it cheers my heart. There is no situation in life, however unpleasant it may be, but has some bright places in it. I love to cheat Mrs. Mills; I watch my chance when she is not near, and let off the cold air in the radiator until the warm air comes, and then close it. I add coal to the fire, saying to myself, "This castle belongs to the Province, and so do I. We have a right to all the comforts of life here, and especially so when five dollars a week is paid for our board; let us have a nice fire and bask in its comforting rays." I love the heat; if the seats at the grate get filled up, I come back to the radiator. Perhaps it is warm enough to afford to have the window open a few moments, to let the impure air escape—just a little of it; then I sit close by it, calling it my kitchen fire-place. I am regulating the comfort of this ward in a measure, but they don't know it.

February.—My dear Lewis has been to see me today. We chat together as usual; how can he think me crazy? Dr. Steeves tells him I am, I suppose, and so he thinks it must be so. He is so happy to see me

looking better; he is more loving than ever; he holds my hand in his and tells me he will take me out for a drive when the weather is fine. And I said, "Oh Lewis, my dear boy, I am well enough to go home with you to your hotel now." I so long for some of Mrs. Burns' good dinners; her meals are all nice, and here we have such horrid stuff. Dark-colored, sour bakers' bread, with miserable butter, constitutes our breakfast and tea; there is oatmeal porridge and cheap molasses at breakfast, but I could not eat that, it would be salts and senna for me. At noon we have plenty of meat and vegetables, indifferently cooked, but we don't require food suitable for men working out of doors. We need something to tempt the appetite a little.

No matter what I say, how earnestly I plead, he believes Dr. Steeves in preference to me. If I should die here, he will still believe Dr. Steeves, who looks so well they cannot think he would do so great a wrong. When I first began to realize that I must stay here all winter, I begged the Doctor to take me to his table, or change his baker; "I cannot live on such fare as you give us here." His reply was, "I don't keep a boarding house." Who does keep this boarding house? Is there any justice on earth or under heaven? Will this thing always be allowed to go on? Sometimes I almost sink in despair. One consolation is left me—some day death will unlock those prison doors, and my freed spirit will go forth rejoicing in its liberty.

There is a dear girl here whose presence has helped to pass the time more pleasantly, and yet I am more anxious on her account. How can her mother leave her so long in such care as this? Ah, they cannot know how she is faring; she often says, "I used to have nice cake at home, and could make it, too." She has been teaching school, has over-worked, had a fever, lost her reason, and came here last June. She is well enough to go home. I fear if they leave her here much longer she will never recover her spirits. She is afraid of Mrs. Mills, and dare not ask for any favor. Mrs. Mills is vexed if she finds her in my room, and does not like to see us talking. I suppose she fears we will compare notes to her disadvantage, or detrimental to the rules of the house. I think it is against the rules of this house that we should be indulged in any of the comforts of life.

March.—At last I have my trunk: why it should have been detained so long I cannot conceive. I feel rich in the possession of the little needful articles it contains.

I enquired of Dr. Steeves, some time ago, if he had not in the Asylum a supply of necessary articles for our use, telling him I wanted a paper of pins very much. He said they were for the indigent patients, so I got none. My son, Tom, gave me some small silver some weeks ago, but I was no better off. No one would do me an errand outside. I begged Mrs. Mills at different times to buy me some pins, and to buy me an extra quart of milk. I was so hungry for milk, but she said it was against the rules of the house. She gives me now a glass nearly full at bed time, with one soda biscuit. This is the only luxury we have here; some others get the same. It is because I have tried to make her think we are her children, left in her care. I said to her, "'Feed my lambs,' you are our Shepherd;" and she is if she only knew it. I have quoted the words of Him whose example we should all follow: "Do good unto others." I am watching over those poor lambs now, to see how they are tended, and I will tell the Commissioners in whose care the Asylum is left by the Province. The people of New Brunswick suppose they attend to it. The Commissioners have placed it in the care of Dr. Steeves, and they believe him quite capable of conducting it properly. Is this the way it should be done? I don't think so.

I observed Miss Fowler today holding her hand to her eye, which is looking inflamed; she is blind; a well-educated, delicate, gentle-woman. I take more than usual interest in her for that reason. I often sit beside her and she tells me of her mother, and wants me to go home with her to number one. She does not seem a lunatic, and she is neglected. I tied her eye up with my own handkerchief, and a wet rag on it. I did not mean to offend, I had done so before and it was not observed. Mrs. Mills came along just as I had done it; she jerked it off in anger, and threw it on the floor. I said to her, "That is not a Christian act," but she pays no heed; perhaps her morning work makes her feel cross.

I come back to my own room and write again; what shall I do? I cannot—how can I stay here any longer! and I cannot get away, locked in as prisoners in our rooms at night, fed like paupers. If I were committed to the penitentiary for a crime, I would not be used any worse than I am here. My heart longs for sympathy, and has it not. I have tried to soften Mrs. Mills' heart, and win her sympathy, but I cannot, and I cannot withhold my pity for those poor invalids who fare even worse than I.

March 13.—I must write this while fresh in my mind, for fear I may forget. There is a Miss Short here—a fair-haired, nice-looking girl; she stands up

and reads in the Testament as if she were in
Sunday-school, recites poetry, and tries to play on
the piano. I did not think her much out of order
when she came, but she is now. She has grown
steadily worse. Her father came to see her, and she
cried to go home with him. I wished very much to
tell him to take her home, but Mrs. Mills did not
leave them, and I dared not speak to him. She has
grown so much worse, she tears her dress off, so
they have to put leather hand-cuffs on her wrists
so tight they make her hands swell. I say, "Oh, Mrs.
Mills, don't you see they are too tight, her hands
look ready to burst—purple with blood." She paid
no heed: "It does not hurt her any." Yesterday she
tied a canvas belt round her waist so tight that it
made my heart ache to look at it. I am sure it would
have stopped my breath in a short time; they tied
her to the back of the seat with the ends of it.

March 17.—Another poor victim has come to our
ward today—a black-eyed, delicate-looking girl.
She looked *so sad*, I was drawn to her at once. I sat
beside her in Mrs. Mills' absence, and enquired the
cause of her trouble; she said her food gave her
pain—she is dyspeptic. If the Doctor would
question the patients and their friends as to the
cause of their insanity, they might, as in other cases
of illness, know what remedy to apply. This dear
child has been living at Dr. Wm. Bayards' three
years—chambermaid—that is enough to assure me
she is a good girl. I think she wears her dress too
tight. I unloosened her laces and underskirts to

make them easy; they are all neat and tidy, as if
she had come from a good home.

Another day is here. That poor girl is in great
trouble yet. When I went out into the hall this
morning, she was kneeling by the door; she laid her
cheek on the bare floor, praying for her sins to be
forgiven, murmuring something of those who had
gone before. I cannot think she has sinned; poor
child! she has lost her health in some way; she has
transgressed some law of nature. I think it has been
tight lacing that caused some of the trouble, for
she sat up on the floor when I invited her to stand
up for fear some one would open the door and
walk over her, and rubbed the calf of her leg,
saying it was all numb. Anything too tight causes
pain and distress by interrupting the free
circulation of the blood. She is so pitiful and sad!
How could Mrs. Mills speak so unkindly to her,
pushing her with her foot to make her rise up? She
treats them like wicked school-boys who have
done something to torment her and merit
punishment. I cannot but pity Mrs. Mills, for this is
an uncomfortable position to fill, and if she has
always obeyed her Superintendent, she has done
her duty, and deserves a retired allowance. The
younger nurses are all learning from her, and will
grow hard-hearted, for they think she is one to
teach them; they come to her for help in case of
emergency, and they go all together, and are able
to conquer by main strength what might in most
cases be done by a gentle word. "A soft answer
turneth away wrath;" I have known this all my life,
but I never felt it so forcibly as now.

There is a lady here from Westmoreland; her hair is cut short, and her eyes are black and wild. The first time I spoke to her she struck me, lightly, and I walked away; I knew she was crazy. After I had met her a few times and found she was not dangerous, I ventured to sit down beside her. She was lying on her couch in a room off the dining-room; she lay on her back knitting, talking in a rambling way: "Do you know what kind of a place this is? Aren't you afraid I'll kill you? I wish I was like you." I smoothed her hair with my hand as I would a child. I thought, perhaps, she had done some great wrong. She said she had killed her mother. Often before, I had stood beside her, for I looked at her a number of times before I ventured to sit by her. I had no recollection of seeing her when I first came, till I found her in this room. I suppose she was so violent they shut her in here to keep her from striking or injuring any one. I could not discover the cause of her trouble, but I comforted her all I could, and she has always been friendly with me since, and listened to my words as if I were her mother. She has been here a long time. Last Friday— bathing day—two young, strong nurses were trying to take her from her room to the bath-room (I suppose she was unwilling to be washed, for I have noticed when I saw her in that room on the couch, she was not clean as she should be—her clothes did not have a good air about them). The nurses were using force, and she struggled against it. They used the means they often use; I suppose that is their surest method of conquering the obstinate spirit that will rise up to defend itself in any child or woman. She was made more violent by her hair being pulled; one nurse had her hands, and the other caught her by her hair, which is just long enough to hold by. They made her walk. I was walking near them when I saw one seize her by the hair; she tried to bite her on the arm. I started forward, and laid my hand on her arm, with—"Don't, my poor child, don't do so; be gentle with her, girls, and she will go." She looked at me, and her face softened; that angry spirit melted within her, and they went on to the bath-room. Shortly after that I met her looking fresh and nice; she was in Mrs. Mills' room, in her rocking-chair. Sometimes I look in there to see if that chair is empty, to have a rock in it myself. I think it better for her health to knit in the rocking-chair than to lay down and knit or read either, so I leave her there. Perhaps she has read too much and injured her brain; if so, I would not let her read so much.

March 20.—Poor Mrs. Mills has served thirty-two years here, and has become hardened as one will to any situation or surroundings. She is too old a woman, and her temper has been too much tried. She is tidy, and works well for so old a woman, but

she is not fit for a nurse. If she were a British
soldier, and had served her country so long, she
would be entitled to a pension.

Poor Miss Short! Last week I saw her lying on the
floor nearly under the bed, her dress torn, her hair
disheveled. How can her friends leave her so long!
Some ladies came to see her a short time ago, and
as they left the hall I heard her call them to take
her with them. If they knew all as I do, they would
not leave her here another day.

There is a Miss Snow here from St. Stephens. I
remember distinctly when I first came, she raved
all the time. I did not dare to look in her bed-room.

I must write something of myself today. I can look
back and see plainly all my journey here. The day
may come when I shall be laid away in the grave,
and my boys—the dear boys I have loved so well—
will look over my trunk and find this manuscript;
they will then perhaps believe I am not crazy. I
know Dr. Steeves tells them I am a lunatic yet. They
will weep over this, as they think of the mother
they have left here to die among strangers. It
would be happiness to die surrounded by my
friends, to be able to tell them they have only to
live well that they may die well. To be true to
ourselves and to our fellows, is all the good we
need. That I have always striven to do, does now
my spirit feed.

I have been so near the grave, the border land of
heaven. I heard angels' voices; they talked with me

even as they did with John on the Isle of Patmos, when they said to him, "Worship God who sent me."

I was very much alone, engaged in writing a book on the laws of health. My desire to write increased; I became so absorbed with my work I forgot to eat, and, after a day or two, I seemed to think I had done some wrong. The angel voices whispered me that I must fast and pray; I know I had plenty of food in my closet, but I don't remember eating any more. I fasted eight days, and felt comfortable and happy most of the time. I sang to myself, "O death, where is thy sting, where is thy victory, boasting grave." I wept for my own sins, and wished to die, the world to save. I was trying to perform some ancient right or vow, one day, and my sons came in. I ordered them away, but they would not go. They said they would bring me home, for Lewis, who was living with me near Boston, sent for my son, T. M. Pengilly, who is proprietor of a drug store in St. John. I suppose he discovered I was fasting, and saw me failing so fast he telegraphed to Tom to come to his assistance. I remember I kissed him when he came, asked him what he came for, and bade him leave me. I know now how unreasonable that was, for we had no other room but Lewis' bed-room, and in it there was no fire. We had rented rooms, as Lewis took his meals at a boarding-house near. Poor boys, they went in and out; it seemed to me they did not eat or sleep for some days; I thought they were as crazy as I was in the cars.

They brought Dr. Hunter to see me. I had been
acquainted with him some time previous. I told him
I was sorry they had brought him to see me, for I
needed no physicians, I only needed to fast and
pray. "I know you are a good man, Dr. Hunter, but
you need not come to see me again; I will be all
right in time; God and His angels will keep me
always." These were my words to him; I know not
what prompted me; I suppose it was my insanity. I
think I told them to nail up the doors and leave me
there till summer. That was the last week of
October. My poor boys, how tried and worried they
must have been. They watched me night and day
alternately. I told them I had not talked with them
enough of my own religion. I begged Tom to read
the Bible and kneel and pray, but he would not; I
think he fell asleep in my rocking-chair (how often I
have wished for that rocking-chair since I came
here).

On Sunday morning I heard them say, "We will go
home in the first train." Lewis went out to see
about it, and I told Tom I wished to take the
sacrament, and he should give it to me, for he
would yet be bishop of St. John—"St. Thomas" he
should be called. I can but laugh when I think of it
now, but it was very real to me then. I had been a
member—a communicant—of St. James' Church,
Episcopal, some years; I had taken my boys to
Sunday School, to receive that religious instruction
which I was not qualified to give. They had
accompanied me to church, always, but I felt as if I
had not spoken to them on religious subjects as I
ought to have done.

It is fourteen years, I think, since I was christened in St. James' Church, by Rev. William Armstrong, whose voice I always loved to hear in the beautiful service of our church. I was confirmed by Bishop John Fredricton, in Trinity Church. I well remember the pressure of that reverend hand upon my head, and the impressive words of his address to us who were that day received into the church—"Let your inner life be as good or better than your outer life, if you would be worthily known as His children." He desired the young men in particular to take up some useful study, to occupy their leisure hours—something outside of their every-day business of life. What better words could have been said; I would that the young men of the present day should often hear those words and accept them as a rule of their life. I float away from thoughts of my insanity to the days when I was at home going to church with my children. I must return to my subject.

They brought the table to my bedside; I kept my eyes closed; I received the bread from the hand of one son, and the wine from the hand of the other. I tasted it, and my fast was broken. I discovered, to my great surprise, it was only toast and tea. They had improved upon my wish, and thought to feed me, their poor wasted mother. They dressed me for the journey; I would not assist them any; they had not obeyed my wish to be left alone in my room all winter; so, when I yielded to them, I left all for them to do; the only thing I did myself was to take from the closet this grey flannel dress—I had made it for traveling, before I left Lowell for

Old Orchard. They did not seem to know what they were doing. I had two bonnets, but they never mentioned them, as I remember. They left my night-cap on, and tied a silk handkerchief over it. They carried me down stairs in their arms, and lifted me in the coach. After we were on our way in the cars, I found my hair was hanging down my back; I had nothing to fasten it up with, and I arranged the handkerchief to cover it. I began to feel happy with the thought of going home. I tried to cheer them, and they could not help smiling at me. I wondered they were not ashamed of me, I looked so badly. I told them not to call me mother, to say I was old Mrs. Sinnett; that they were bringing me home to my friends.

Poor boys, I wonder if they remember that journey in the cars as I do. At my request, Tom brought me a goblet of milk, at two stopping places, and when I found they had brought me to an Asylum I felt no fear; I thought I had only to ask and receive what I needed. I knew they thought me crazy, so I would not bid them good-bye, when they left me, but concluded to play lunatic. I refused to kiss Lewis when he left me, that dear boy who had watched over me so faithfully, carrying me in his arms from one car to the other. When we changed cars, he placed me in a Pullman car, and I thought I was safely hidden from something, I knew not what. I only know I was so happy while I was with my sons; nothing troubled me. I sang and chatted to Lewis; he would not leave me a moment; he kneeled beside my berth, and I called him my best of sons, and smoothed his hair with my hand. All my journey through I heard the voice of angels whispering to me, "Hold on by the hand of your sons; keep them with you and you will be safe; they are your sons, they are the sons of God,"— and they are. All who do their duty as they were doing, to the best of their ability, are the children of God; for, if we do the best we can, angels can do no more.

I thought I was perfectly safe here, and if the Doctor had given me the food which should be given to an invalid, or if he had granted any requests I made to him in a reasonable manner, I should not have been prompted to write these lines or recall those memories of the past.

One thought brings another. When, on the morning after my arrival, I begged for milk and biscuit, they refused, and then brought a bowl of common looking soup with black looking bakers' bread. I refused to eat it; if it had been beef tea with soda biscuit in it, I would have taken it myself. They did not live to coax crazy people. Mrs. Mills called in her help, and it did not need many, I was so weak; they held me back, and she stuffed the soup down my throat.

When I came here first, I told the nurse my name was Mary Huestis; that was my maiden name; I hardly know why I prefer that to my sons' name, for they are sons no mother need be ashamed of. My prayers for them have always been, that they might be a benefit to their fellows; that they grow to be good men; to be able to fill their places in the world as useful members of society, not living entirely for themselves, but for the good of others, an honor to themselves and a blessing to the world. If we live well, we will not be afraid to die. "Perfect love casteth out fear." I must write no more today.

March 24.—Two years ago today I was watching by the bedside of my dying child. Driven from our home by the fire, I was tarrying for her to complete her education in the city of Lowell, which is second to no city in the world for its educational privileges. Free schools, with books free to all its children, and excellent teachers. To Lowell schools and to my darling child, I must here pay this tribute. The day after her death, the principal of the school she attended addressed the school with these words— "Clara Pengilly has attended this school two years, and I have never heard a fault found with her; there has never been a complaint brought to me by

teacher or schoolmates concerning her." Her teacher brought me two large bouquets to ornament the room at her funeral, sent by the pupils and teachers of the school where she had been a happy attendant, for she loved her teachers, and always told me how good and kind they were to her; no wonder every one loved her, for she had a loving heart and a nature so full of sunshine she could not be unhappy. We had boarded eight months with a lady whose only daughter was blind from her birth. Clara loved to lead her out for a walk, and read to her at home; no pleasure was complete unless shared with her blind friend, who was younger than herself, and whose life she could brighten by her willingness to devote her unoccupied time to her service. Dear Lorelle, we all loved her for her goodness, and pitied her for her infirmity. The boarders and others at her home sent flowers too. Her mother arranged a green vine and flowers around her face and in her hand. When she had finished, she said, "That is the last we can do for you, Clara; I know she was so fond of flowers, she would be pleased if she could see them." I cared not for the flowers, I only knew that loving heart was stilled in death, and I was left alone; with an effort, I said, "Lorelle will never know a truer friend than she who lies here." My tears unbidden flow; why do I go back in memory to those sorrowful days? I know she is happy now. Let me draw the veil of charity over the past with all its troubles, remembering only the many acts of kindness done for us by our friends at that time.

It is this waiting so long a prisoner, begging to be liberated. My hands will not remain folded or my brain idle. I must write again of poor Miss Snow. I ventured into her room, feeling anxious to help her by coaxing her into a better frame of mind. She is wasted to a shadow; I am sure if she had any food to tempt her to eat she would grow stronger; some nice bread and milk at bed time would help her to sleep. I soothed her as I would a child in trouble, until she ceased her raving, and then questioned her to discover the cause of her disease. She is a well-educated, intelligent lady. In her ravings she often says she is the only lady in the hall, and seems to have a temper of her own, which has been made more than violent by her stay in this ward. She is very fond of drawing small pencil sketches, and works at them late at night, which I think is certainly injurious. I conclude she is the victim of late hours and fancy work; she acknowledges she used to sew until after twelve, working for bazaars. If the ladies would only come here and study the needs of these poor victims of insanity, and make better arrangements for their welfare, they would find a higher calling than exhausting their energies working for bazaars, and leaving us to the care of those who care nothing for us and will not learn. Too much temper and too much indolence rule here. I go in sometimes and coax her to stop talking and lie down. I cover her up to keep her warm; she is blue with the cold. If I could keep her in a nice warm room, with kind treatment and nourishing food! She could not eat that horrible, sour bakers' bread with poor butter. Sometimes her food would set in her room a long time. I guess she only eats when she is so starved she can't help it. I eat because I am determined to live until I find some one who will help me out of this castle on the hill, that I may tell the Commissioners all about it. Sometimes I term it a college, in which I am finishing my education, and I shall graduate some day—when will it be? My impatient spirit chafes at this long delay. I sit at the grated window and think, if I were one of those little pigeons on the window sill I would be happy; content to be anything if only at liberty.

April.—The friends of Miss Short have been here and taken her home, and word returned that she is better. I am thankful to think she is with her mother, and I do not see her so improperly treated; it made me feel wretched to think of her.

Poor Katy Dugan's friends came one day. I watched my chance and told one of them to let her mother know she was getting worse and was not well treated. I had many heart-aches for that girl; I scarcely know why. They must have seen she looked worse; her dress of flannel, trimmed with satin of the same color, which looked so nice when she came, was filthy with spots of gruel and milk they had been forcing her to eat. This day, I remember, was worse than common days of trouble. I had been excited by seeing one of the most inoffensive inmates pushed and spoken to very roughly, without having done any wrong. They attempted to comb that poor girl's hair; she will

not submit, begs and cries to go down there. I go to
the bath-room door to beg them to be gentle with
her. Mrs. Mills slammed the door in my face. She is
vexed at any expression of sympathy. Again I hear
that pitiful cry, and I go up the hall to see what the
trouble is. They had taken her in a room to hold her
on the floor, by those heavy, strong nurses sitting
on her arms and feet, while they force her to eat. I
return, for I can't endure the sight. I met Mrs. Mills,
with a large spoon, going to stuff her as she did me.
(I was not dyspeptic; I had fasted and would have
eaten if they had given me milk, as I requested.)
She was angry at me again; she ordered me to my
room, and threatened to lock me in. What have I
done to merit such treatment? How can I endure
this any longer!

April 3.—Yesterday was election day of the
Aldermen of the city of St. John. Dr. Steeves came
in this morning and congratulated me very
pleasantly that my son was elected Alderman. I
thanked him and said I was not at all surprised, for
he was very popular in his ward; always kind and
courteous to every one, he had made many

friends. He must know I am perfectly sane, but I can't persuade him to tell my son I am well enough to go home.

My dear Lewis has gone eight hundred miles beyond Winnipeg surveying. I am sorry to have him go so far. Will I ever see him again? But I feel so badly when he comes to see me, and refuses to take me home with him; and I say to myself, "I would die here alone rather than that he, my darling boy, should be shut in here and treated as I am;" for his temper, if so opposed, would make him a maniac. I have dreamed of seeing him looking wretched and crying for fresh air, for he was suffocating. All the time I had those troubled dreams, I was smothering with gas coming in my room through the small grating intended to admit heat to make us comfortable, but it did not. I was obliged to open the window to be able to breathe; my lungs required oxygen to breathe when I was lying in bed, not gas from hard coal.

There is one lady whose room is carpeted and furnished well, but she is so cold she sits flat on the carpet beside the little grate, trying to be warm. She has not enough clothing on to keep her warm. Her friends call often, but they never stay long enough to know that her room is cold. They cannot know how uncomfortable she is, or what miserable food she has, for we all fare alike.

April is nearly gone. Tom has promised to come for me on Monday; I feel so happy to think I am going to be free once more. I sat on my favorite seat in the window sill, looking at those poor men working on the grounds. There were three; they did not look like lunatics, no overseer near them; they were shoveling or spading, and three ducks followed them. Fed by the All-Father's hand, they gather food for themselves; the men never disturb them; they cannot be violent. Many a farmer would be willing to give one of those men a permanent home for his services. The knowledge that this home is here for them to return to, would ensure them kind treatment at the hand of the farmer, and I am sure they would prefer life on a farm, with good palatable food and liberty, to being shut up here as prisoners and fed as paupers, as we in the ladies' ward are, without one word or look of sympathy or respect extended to us.

One day this week, I had been watching one of the men working at the strawberry beds, thinking I would like to live on a farm now, that I might cultivate those lovely berries. The Doctor came in to make his usual morning call, in the hall, with a book and pencil in his hand; that is all he ever does for us. I thought I would make him think I thought him a gentleman, which he is not, and perhaps he would be more willing to let me go home. It has taken effect. I suppose he thinks I have forgotten all the doings of the past winter, and that I will not dare to say anything against such a mighty man as he is. I am glad I have taken it down in black and white, so as not to forget the wrongs of the Province, and the wrongs of those poor neglected women, of whom I am one. I ought not to write in this manner, but my indignation overcomes me sometimes, and I cannot help it. He is a little more social now than usual, and I suggest that if he bring blackberry bushes from the field, and set them around the fence, keeping the ground irrigated round the roots, he might have as nice fruit as the cultivated. He said yes, he would send some of his men out to his farm and get some, and he left as pleasant as he came. That was the first time he ever left me without being driven away by my making some request, and being refused.

This reminds me of the day I begged so hard for a pot of Holloway's Ointment. I had asked my boys several times to bring it to me, and I thought they always forgot it. I had used it many years, not constantly, only for a little rash on my face at times; it has annoyed me very much lately. This day I had urged him all I could, and he left me, saying he had too much on his mind today. I followed him to the door, saying, "I don't want to think so ill of you, Doctor, as that you will not grant me so small a favor—a twenty-five cent favor—and I will pay for it myself."

Saturday Morning.—I am so impatient! I hardly dare to hope. Will I be free to breathe the air of heaven again, to walk out in the warmth of His sunshine? Perhaps I am punished for questioning the exact truth of that story, so long ago, that I could not quite explain to myself or believe how it could be handed down over so many years. I have stood almost where He has stood, once before in my life. "The foxes have holes, and the birds of the air have nests, but the Son of man hath not where to lay his head." I have been "led by the spirit into the wilderness." Pontius Pilate is not here to say, "I find no sin in this man," but there are those here who would lock me in, and never let me set my foot outside of these walls, if they knew I was writing this with the hope of laying it before the Province.

Yesterday was bathing-day—a cold, damp April day. No steam on; I tried the radiators, but there was no hot air to come. The young teacher—in whom I was so much interested, and whose name I will not give here, as she always begged me not to mention her name—she stood with me at the radiator trying to find some heat. The Doctor came in and I say, "Doctor, can't you send up some coal, there is only a few red coals in the grate, no steam on, and we are nearly frozen?" He said, "The hard coal is all gone." "Well, send us some soft coal, wood, anything to keep us warm." He left us; no coal came till after dinner. I met one of the nurses in the next ward; I told her our wants, and she sent it by a young man who was always attentive and respectful, but we could not always find a messenger who would take the trouble to find him.

The Doctor has been in again: Mary and I were together as usual. He looked at us very pleasantly, and I said, "You will be able to send us home now soon, surely." He drew me away from her, saying, "I don't wish her to hear this. Don't you know, Mr. Ring went to Annapolis and hung himself?" "They did not watch him well," said I, and he left, thinking, I suppose, that he had silenced me effectually. I went to Mrs. Mills, and enquired about Mr. Ring, and learned that he had never been here, and was quite an old man. What had that to do with us? We have no wish to harm ourselves or any one else. I see now that is the influence he uses to induce people to leave their friends here. My son told me one day he had kept the Asylum so well the public were perfectly satisfied with him; no wonder he conducts it so well when there are so few lunatics here. I suppose he has left me here waiting for me to get satisfied too; well, I am, but as soon as I am out I shall write to Mary's mother to come for her, for I can hardly go and leave her here. I have taken her in my heart as my own; she is so good a girl, wasting her precious life here for the amusement of others—I don't see anything else in it.

St. John's Hotel, April 30.—At last I am free! Seated in my own room at the hotel, I look back at that prison on the hill. I had won a little interest in the hearts of the nurses in our ward; they expressed regret at my leaving. Ellen Regan, who was the first to volunteer me any kindness, said, "We shall miss you, Mrs. Pengilly, for you always had a cheerful word for every one." I did not bid all the patients good-bye, for I hope soon to return and stay with them. I would like so much to look after these poor women, who are so neglected. I will ask the Commissioners to allow me to remain with them, if only one year, to superintend the female department, not under the jurisdiction of the present Superintendent, but with the assistance of the Junior Physician and the nurses, who each understand the work of their own departments, and will be willing to follow my instructions. I will teach them to think theirs is no common servitude—merely working for pay—but a higher responsibility is attached to this work, of making comfortable those poor unfortunates entrusted to their care, and they will learn to know they are working for a purpose worth living for; and they will be worthy of the title, "Sisters of Mercy."

Tuesday.—I have been to the Solicitor-General, and left with him a copy of parts of my diary, and I am prepared to attest to its truth before the Board of Commissioners, whenever it shall meet. He said he was pleased to have my suggestions, as they now had the Provincial Lunatic Asylum under consideration, and assured me he would attend to it. His words and manners assure me he is a gentleman to be relied on, and I feel safe in leaving my case in his hands.

June.—I have spent three weeks in Fredericton, the capital of New Brunswick, while waiting for the Board of Commissioners to meet and discuss the affairs of the Provincial Lunatic Asylum, concerning which my time at present is devoted. They are members of Government, and seem to be too busy for anything. I called on the Attorney-General, with what effect he himself best knows; it is not worth repeating here. I will only say, neither he nor his partner quite understand the courtesy due to a woman or lady. It cannot be expected of persons who are over-loaded with business, that they shall have leisure sufficient to oversee the arrangements of the Provincial Lunatic Asylum, which needs, like any other household, a woman's care to make it perfect.

In my wanderings since the fire of 1877, I boarded some weeks at the Y. W. C. A. home in Boston, a beautiful institution, conducted entirely by ladies. It was a comfortable, happy home, ruled by ladies who were like mothers or friends to all its occupants, and under the supervision of a committee of ladies who visit it every week. It is such arrangements we need to perfect the working of our public institutions, where a woman's care is required as in a home. Men are properly the outside agents, but women should attend to the inner working of any home.

The Tewksbury affair of 1883, stands a disgrace to the New England States, who had so long prided themselves on their many public charitable institutions, and which have, without question, been an honor to her people.

I am sorry to say they are not all perfect, as I learned from the lips of a young man in this hotel, who looked as if he were going home to die. He had been waiting some weeks in the Boston City Hospital, until the warm weather should make his journey less dangerous in his weak state. "If I should live a hundred years, I should never get that hospital off my mind," were his words, as he lay back in his chair looking so sad; "a disagreeable, unkind nurse, a cold ward, and miserable food." His words touched a responsive chord in my heart, for my experiences had been similar to his; I can never forget them.

Let me here entreat the ladies, wherever this book may be read, that they take this work upon themselves. Rise up in your own strength, and solicit the Governor to appoint you as Commissioners, as you are over your Old Ladies' Homes. If the Governor has the authority or power to appoint those who now form the Board of Commissioners of the Provincial Lunatic Asylum, he can surely invest you with the same title, and you will not any longer allow your fellow-sisters to be neglected by those who cannot understand the weakness or the misfortunes that have brought them under the necessity of being protected by the public.

Before leaving Fredericton, I called at the Government House to lay my case before His Excellency the Lieutenant Governor, hoping to awaken his sympathy in our cause, and urge him to call an early meeting of the Board. I was so anxious to return to the care of those poor feeble women I had left in the Asylum; so anxious to right their wrongs, I could not be restrained by friend or foe from finishing this work so near my heart. Some of my friends really believe me insane on the subject. There are those who can apply this to themselves, and others whose kindness and hospitality I shall ever remember with grateful pleasure. They will none of them doubt the truth of this statement.

Governor Wilmot did not doubt me. He received me very kindly, as did also his good lady. After conversing with him on the subject until I felt I ought not trespass any longer on his time, I rose to leave, and at the door expressed a wish for a bunch of lilacs that grew in great abundance on large bushes interspersed with trees, and which made the grounds look very beautiful. He gathered me a bunch with his own hand, for which I felt thankful and highly honored; as we walked together I told him my father's name. "Lewis Huestis," said he, "I knew him well." I had not known that, but I did know that Wilmot had always been an honored name in my father's house. When bidding him good-bye, I again referred to the old subject, by saying, "I have lost my home and business by the fire; my sons are scattered abroad in the world and do not need my care; I would like to devote my remaining years, as far as I am able, to better the condition of those poor sufferers in the Asylum." He answered, "I hope you will, for I think it will be well for them to have your care, and I will do all I can to assist you." These were his words, as near as I can remember, and I left the Government House, feeling as if I had been making a pleasant call on an old friend. I write these last few lines as a tribute of respect to the memory of the name of Governor Wilmot, and that of my own father, who always had the interests of his country at heart.

I returned to the city feeling cheered by the words of encouragement and sympathy I had received. It well repaid me for the trouble of my journey to Fredericton.

I will leave this subject now in the hands of the ladies, wherever this little book may find them, who, having leisure and influence, will not, I hope, fail to use them for the benefit of suffering humanity, remembering we are all children of one Father—Our Father in Heaven. Improve the talent He has given you, that it may be said to you, "Well done, thou good and faithful servant."

Respectfully, M. H. P.

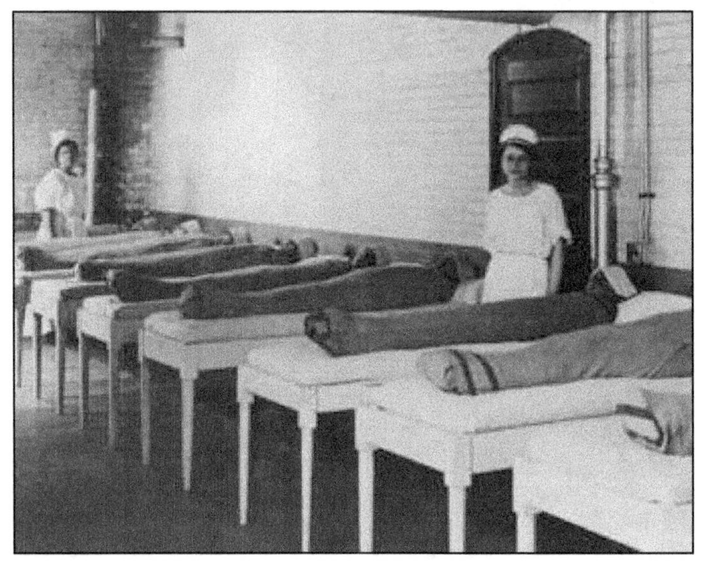